Bodies of Time and Space

Bodies of Time and Space

Poems by

Glen A. Mazis

Cover design by Shay Culligan
Cover image from IStock

ISBN: 978-1-63980-195-4

Kelsay Books
502 South 1040 East, A-119
American Fork, Utah 84003
Kelsaybooks.com

Acknowledgments

Burningwood Poetry Journal: "The Sri Lankan with the Scar Across His Cheek"

Ellipsis: "The Male Ambivalence to Moonlight"

Gone, But Not Forgotten: "Bhakti, the Zen Chihuahua"

Olentangy Review: "The Printer Who Lost His Words"

The Poet's Guild: "The Naked Oyster's Rondeau Redoublé"

Quiet Diamonds: "The Body's Arrival," "The Natural Power of Memory" "The Gustatory Zeal of Falling Snow," "Élan Vital Proliferates"

Reed Magazine: "The True Dimensions of the Body"

Rosebud: "Falling Echoes"

Sangam Literary Magazine: "The Body Between Us," "Our First Glance at the Light," "Matter Misrepresented," "City Walking on a Hot August Night"

Spoon River Poetry Review: "In Defense of Habit"

Orchard Street Press published the chapbook *The Body Is a Dancing Star,* which includes: "The Body's Arrival," "Our Bodies at Rest," "The Face of the World Sees Itself," "In Defense of Habit," "When Maps Won't Help," "Losing Our Ground," "Word Mother Working Long," "The Male Ambivalence Toward Moonlight," "Michelangelo's Confession," "Matter Misrepresented," "Matter's Many Faces," "Hummingbirds Signal the Evolution of Mind," "Our First Glance at the Light," "Thomas Hobbes Denies Perception's Sense," "The Torn Ozone Layer," "No Time for Goodbyes," "The Hunted Demon Is the Most Social Animal," "The Wolf Asks, Who Is the Demon?" "The Natural Power of Memory," "Speaking the Same Language," "Seals Sail by All Day at Cape Cod," "The Body of the One I Love," "The Body Between Us"

Contents

I. Vulnerable Bodies

I. Vulnerable Bodies

The Body's True Dimensions

An arm and a galaxy might
begin to make a body,
or the cinders of old volcanos
might become the soles of our feet
if the embers still glow.

Our bodies stretch so far
we need to add a dimension
to the map of the world
where they might live
and lie seeded in together
like the juicy insides
of pomegranates.

The ear awakens each day
to the sound of the silent Buddha
sitting under the Bo tree
and within this soft flesh
everything else sounds a note
rings the resonating bell
sits on a brightly colored
circular pillow
of the whole body.

A back and a mountain
might reach up to the shoulders
of the clouds that cross the sky
offering our minds a path
to slip down towards the end
or rest our heavy loads on
those blue stretched sinews.

We can then bend down
from these concerned heights
to lie across the earth
and sleep quietly in the fold
of the arm that cradles.

The Body's Arrival

The body is the world's way
of welcoming flesh to open
for streams and salamanders,
the world's way of adding weight
to weightless spirit,
each object seen or felt
encircling a place to be ours.

Invited into the silence
of the night
the body expands to find
others of its kind
dark flashes burn
beneath the skin,
entangled limbs spin
the same release.

Only for a being with hands
do fish and birds swim
soar through minds
landing against the rooted tree
finding a way over tops
of sky only to burrow
into roots gnarled
with memory.

The straightened back gives
altitude to thoughts
who face to face
address cliffs of slate,
as hearts squeeze
like sea anemones
becoming abandoned hives
where the world's
creatures hide.

15

His Body Files for Divorce

His body once left him,
got an apartment in a run-down
        part of town,
wouldn't answer his desperate
        telephone calls
considered joining forces with
        another man,
excitedly fantasized of melding perhaps
        with an appreciative woman.

The body was cross, no, irate
finally answering the phone
        one lazy late Sunday morning
lying in bed with a sumptuous breakfast.
        You never got it.
I was you, all the way.
        You were nothing without me.
He didn't know what to say
        he thought his body was merely useful.

It was ridiculous being shut up
in his big house just floating around
        not able to sense anything
bumping into ceilings as his hifalutin
        thoughts pushing him ever higher
while he was starving for any meal
        any light touch on his back
and his thoughts were nothing anyway
        puffballs of spirit without a tongue.

Of course, his body was growing fat,
abandoned to an endless array of desires
        to eat, to see, to feel, to indulge
slave to those things so seductively appealing
        his mind had vetoed with its sane
reason about limits and good health
        being so cautious, obligated always,
to consider why's and future consequences
        while his body dallied at an eternal party.

At first, his mind was overjoyed at the prospect
that without that bothering body always
        waylaying beautifully blossoming ideas
it could fly about on the wildest flights of fancy
        without being weighed down by the newest
exciting sensation upsetting its balletic mental
        grace with bulletins informing it of others
about whom it should refocus its energetic concern
        and pay attention to the material world.

Now, his mind was assailed by worries that without
the weight of the flesh hugging the earth closely
        getting lost in embrace with so many beings
communicating by sound and sight and smell
        weaving threads that tied it to so many things
suddenly it couldn't count or calculate or conceive,
        felt hopelessly lost, severed from everything,
the mind dreaded its swirling, no longer held
        it might whoosh away ever higher into space.

A panicked telegram from his mind to his senses
pleads for them to at least send some data or a map
     of where things were and how to find friends,
family, and fresh faces to spark some new ideas
     for even its thoughts were slowing down and
growing dim without the electric jolt of sounds,
     the languorous embrace of smells, the enlivening
splash of colors and the snuggling in with warmth,
     but the senses protest they are too dense
     to be sent by a wire.

The mind finally laments, maybe I had too high an opinion
     of myself, an adolescent pride that I needed to be on my own,
now I want to be part of the pink dogwood
     blossoms' sight and smell and be part of Spring
or soar through the speckled cumulus sky by riding
     on backs of birds whose flapping wings are felt
within fleshy arms and running along the spine,
     to belong to this vast family of material things
         and creatures.

Our Bodies at Rest

The arm that holds your body in orbit with mine
your enveloping breasts against my chest
steadies us on the plane of the earth.

The head drooping on the pillow whispers
night songs that linger in our hearts making
the day follow incantations of moving dreams.

The leg leading up towards your torso slips
into a labyrinth of our desires curling
over mine to kindle our way of joining.

The hand lightly enlaced in my fingers
moves along with mine to signal
silent gestures of slumbering love.

The Body Does

The body puts me among things,
welcomes mornings as beginnings
the way things will get done
or happen to those who wait
longingly for lovers,
for those who suffer in bare rooms
or crouch where their houses
were before the hurricane
or in bombed-out cities,
moments pushing the body
to open or close
as skin and bones
are events we feel.

The body reaches needing,
looks through windows
seeing distance beyond
towards what it can get
meets a world
light or dark
gets itself moving
a gesture written on air
of too many messages.

When Maps Won't Help

There is that one turn in the road
when you know all is unfamiliar,
rocks not quite reddish brown enough,
the trees a bit too thin,
the man on the porch looks away
from your eyes searching the sky,
and you wonder
should I turn back,
or slide from a faraway place
to faraway place
where I might become a new person
forgotten by all those in my town,
like a big storm that was black and heavy
but blew to another state
to release its burden.

If you are the man on the porch,
it may be that you see in those eyes
a searching for the right road
gazing at a sky that is too distant,
someone you knew
who passed the point
of getting home again
with too many whiskey bottles
littering his place, too many times
declaring reform,
gone tomorrow floating down the street,
lost in boozy dreams of the past
when beaten down by a dad
too hazy to embrace,
not even solid enough to push
him away on his own path.

So many saving revelations
revolve around his eyes
like headlines in light bulbs
streaming forever around
the first floor of a skyscraper,
but it has no foundation,
can't be condemned or demolished,
can't raze the hurt at the bottom
to give a base to rebuild.
When he asks for a handout
for yet another beginning,
others know
but don't say
he's too far down the road
to make it back to town.

The Sri Lankan with a Scar Across His Cheek

Through the glass doors,
at the back of the house,
she saw you dancing in the air
by the maples, at the
slanting gentle evening hour,
the day after you died.

You had insisted upon making love to her
when she came home with scars
where her lovely breasts had been.
It's important to say they were lovely
because you were
and so was she and
you thought her scarred chest was too.

You always laughed at being the dark,
exotic stranger, the foreigner.
Their theories embraced the Other,
but your brown skin they secretly despised.
Speaking their tongue better,
your colleagues envied a playwriting,
motorcycling Sri Lanken
who knew the French hifalutin books
better than they. Humbug, heartache—
they said you were remote.

You did lay on an Oxford accent
you picked up
in a half hour at Heathrow,
and despite the socialist rap,
strutted a bearing so regal,
you could be cast in a Kipling tale,
but the lines of students
were outside your door,

since uncommon mornings of mist
sticking to hills were in your eyes,
and your voice intoned prayers
for their kind of happiness,
so it might dance with yours.

In a cloud of fire, you rode up to my house
on a new roaring motorcycle.
Hadn't seen you in months,
but you swooped up my woman
and took her careening
through Amish farmlands,
faster than she could breathe,
yellow machine outracing the hues
of yellow wildflowers,
so she came at eighty miles per.

Your last words while leaving school
for the weekend were I know
my body and the pain in my chest
is just too much life,
screeching yellow,
so I need to paint myself
across the tan, black,
and white skins of women,
finding my own line
to ride breezes of the night
in a Buddhist concentration,
while longing to dance in the air.

In Defense of Habit

Freud thought habit stretched across the past
pulling it so tight that when we run away
it's like stomping on a trampoline
that bounces us head over heel
into a dizzy future
where my dead father who wouldn't
talk to me on the phone during his last decade
still curls my lips with his lisp,
so each time I say my w's
I am tripped up by a sad inner Elmer Fudd.

Habit is seen as a lime twig, even though
we'd never use lime twigs anymore
to snare birds so cruelly,
yet we imagine ourselves caught
by who we were, as if free will shuts off,
which is why Nietzsche
took to living on mountain tops,
away from people, not wanting to see
people destroy the child still inside them.

Only Proust saw habit lays its sleepy
head on our lap like our loyal dog,
warding off intruders
and keeping us warm,
nuzzling the past down the right path
through new underbrush. Like Aristotle,
he knew the heft of habit
chisels us until after much work
we find the shape that makes
each accidental dent
a stroke of our particular genius.

The Printer Who Lost His Words

He got to eighty-six as Phil, the printer who could stand
at the press all day, but when he became a man with
a shuffling gait and no words, or very few, his kids
would only call him Frankie. They decided the name
had to fit the man and the printer himself had left
with his words. The hardly used nickname would

signal some other dad was around. The series of strokes
that drove him from the press left the basement
storeroom stacked high with blank sheaves. They
were the telltale signs of an emptiness of a mind
that had lost its lettered substance. Thoughts

became a shushing wind he sucked in through his
cheeks. The wipeout was a by-product of progress,
since in the old days, printers picked out the lead
quads, piece by piece, to set the lines of type. Words
sat on the frame packed in like cars parked on a street.

But with the computerized composers, the words fly
by like the bulletins streaming across the bottom of TV
screens. When the power fails, like the arteries in the
head shutting off for even seconds, the screen blanks
and the words disappear. You can see that in their eyes.

When in past days some lead quads had fallen, someone
could still make out the line, and knew the fallen pieces
were somewhere underfoot. Of course, certain quads
had become almost stuck together, after following one
another so often, like t after s or t after n, that they could

be found in one swoop of the hand and that helped
the lines stay composed, even after spills. The week
after Phil's stroke, Millie, terrified after 60 years
of leaning in the frame against him, went to sleep and
didn't awaken in the morning, fearing she'd be lost
on a floor where no one would find her. She felt herself

slipping without that other quad up against her body,
and decided it was better to jump first. Frankie
was left in front of a TV screen in a nursing home,
watching bulletins fly by for hours, puzzled
at the jumble, while his own inner screen is dark.

The nurses don't realize that within, he still sees
the faint lines of phosphorescence left by the patterns
of their letters so long enlaced together.

Losing Our Ground

Against all odds, my mother returns to the walking.
When the upright is overthrown, deep doubt channels

under the mind. Against all odds, my mother-in-law seemed about
to return, but she slipped out of this life, quickly like a sudden fall

And we fell, for a mother is the curve of the earth, its steady hold
on who we are, the horizon in which all things seem to shine.

Hard to walk without her alongside since we are always within her.
None of us can stand alone, so when mothers fall away

We remain upright by finding how they still stand within us.

Appalachian Trail Mother's Urn

It is one thing to metaphysically declare we all go back into our
  home
while the things of the world extend a hand to join their needy
  body.

It is another to watch the ashes of one you love billow forth in a
  shining
cloud down the reflecting green flow of water in the swift stream

on a Sunday morning, Spring embraced, after holding hands
  quietly
with the circle of family, sisters, spouses, aunts, uncles, small
  children,

fathers and mothers explaining how this is to be remembered
  forever,
to see the core of particles of the mother who was sink to the
  bottom,

then hug the rocks in a shining white phosphorescent energy beam,
as it slides in the current in flourishes of mingling and welcoming,

while staying compactly within the deeper layers of the limpid
  current,
moving into the without us that slips ahead into the time of all
  others.

Word Mother Working Long

You hang on a subway strap, bobbing off balance,
reading the *Times,* as the subway lurches
into a hole from which only the good return.
Each station is reserved for the righteous
and you are served tea at small tables
on long platforms all along the line.

No woman at mid-century goes it alone,
but you raise us on stolen lettuce, not being
bullied by the scarecrow of a large man.
I watch you leave at 7 a.m. and wait for the bus
at 7 p.m. to glide off down the street,
revealing you behind it, small and beat,

like you're the rabbit appearing from the hat
somewhere you never imagined you'd be.
Each night I sleep in the living room,
you create space for me in the stories of boys
who live in their words. Your gift to me,

worlds in words you forfeited for others
to have places where things wouldn't disappear
in a hat. Decades later, I worry you never saw
behind the bus each night a bigger trick—
from within a cloud of carbon monoxide,
you fashioned for us a breath of love.

Minor Miracles in Manhattan

It is well into December
and the yellow daisies, non-stop begonias,
and hybrid impatience
carefully planted in my mother's flowerboxes
still bloom, looking down
on ABC studios across the street,
even though there has been
a parade of icy days.

Frost greets the early morning
audience lineup for Oprah's show
who keep warm dreaming
of perhaps a gift day
when Oprah showers presents
all over the street
like the first snow of the year.
A few might look up at my mother's terrace
and see blossoms in mid-December
and wonder if that's Oprah's doing.

Yet, it may be my mom
who thrives at eighty-six captivated
by Austen's polished phrases
or whooping at finishing
the Time's crossword
or discovering with gusto
a thick soup at a bistro
who makes the flowers persist
when the crowds shiver.

This is our Mother's Day ritual,
the waving stalks of plants driven
from Central Pennsylvania
to live in the Manhattan skyline
gesturing spring love for mothers
and coming summer,
not realizing family hands in the soil
patting plants into place
might have the power
to dispel winter.

A Father Downstream

Heraclitus never said that we can't step
into the same river twice, since
he had his favorites, floating on
the current, slipping into sleep,
as clouds lie softly on his eyes gazing up
and stroke the lids,
while shades of dream whisper among themselves
like little birds of the soul
who twitter the wisdom of the night.
Rather he said there are ever different
waters always in the same place
like a demon in nightmares
who is each person in the recurring dream
and never leaves the family home.

My father was one of the monsters
who loomed across childhood,
each night asleep, his place
in my recurring dream was taken
by a black silhouette in a trench coat
as I walked out of the safety of school.
A pistol in his hand would slowly swing towards me
like a hinged weathervane
and shoot point blank,
sweat left on my pillowcase,
falling into the cold living room of midnight
where I fitfully slept
after he left us, perhaps taking a boat
down the river
where waters don't return.

The great blue herons on the shore
watch the waters intently for hours
standing a good thirty yards apart.
I wonder watching them
if along the bank in the weeds and rushes,
the eddies, he stands unseen,
wanting only the fish
but not the bother of neighbors
or tending a nest, so he might
flap ever slowly like herons,
teetering into the air
to wait quietly downstream.

The Male Ambivalence Toward Moonlight

The oldest myths say the curve
of a woman's breast
is the pendulous shape of moonlight,
the black radiance become flesh,
swinging in syncopation with the center,
harmonic strings running from wolves
to grain, evergreen to owl, sea
to stone, humming at the pit
of her abdomen.

The male transfixed by her breasts
fears the infant self returning,
but no regression inspires his worship.
It's the kisses of a world offered
he'd rather find without lips open,
so he can fashion its replacement
in his image, rather than lowering his face
to lap at the streams of her body.

Michelangelo's Confession

When Michelangelo confessed he
only followed the desires
of the statue already within
this particular piece of marble
allowing its heart to guide his hands,
its will to push him precisely
to break open stone,
he spoke the common plight
of artists and faithful bodies
that move with each
shift of the wind
from the inner heart of things.

Michelangelo betrayed
the secret society of matter's
inner circle,
those who must play dumb
for the benefit of those who
would resent souls
within all things,
for those humans
who need to claim
to be the only lively spirit
on the planet.

Things lack our respect
unseen in their unique faces,
like this white-grey streaked stone
arriving after eons of journeys
to sit here on this patch
of sandy beach, having found home

after its long dance within the sea,
but it is an invisible journey
to those who see a mere rock,
who stop it and all its companions
in mid-gesture of a sign language,
      beckoning friendship.

Matter Misrepresented

Matter has a bad reputation
as stupid and lifeless,
said to fill up the souls
of the stultified.
Religions make their way
by railing against temptations
somehow craftily conjured
by the hidden genius
of this otherwise idiot stuff.

Matter is seen as an infinity
of infinitesimal machines
racing around, colliding,
getting it right
only by sheer accident,
slipping into wondrous combinations
of synchronous functions
like lighting the day
or turning into energy
or letting water fall from the sky
to speed to where
whatever needs to grow
or winding into the intricate
twirl that guide our cells
in a choreographed dance.
Yes, it is admitted, matter does
this, but it's all sevens,
dumb dice rolls.

Of course, science loves matter,
declaring its tracings are the letters
of a numbered language
efficiently removing
all blurry things like love

or beauty from the midst
of its Spartan equations.
Science recruits little soldiers
in perfect formations
to be its messengers,
yet never notices beneath
the starched uniforms
it has a regiment of palimpsests.

Accurately expressing how atoms
become love and life requires
racing pulses, holding hands,
sharing of food
and lying down together
in electrifying bursts,
or else what burns
in their marrow is mistaken
as the arson of billions
of malicious chemical imps
who steal our souls
when we give our hearts away.

Matter is a cosmic calligrapher
transcribing every movement
we make in colored bodies
of every shape opening
in flowerlike petals
while keeping a steady hand
to draw filigrees in our brains
recording the paths of each and every
feeling and thought
left within us
as also within
the circle of the world.

Matter's Many Faces

Maybe matter is like the stone
speaking in silence of breath,
an unmoving face or a tolerance of all.
Maybe matter as water sings
in burbles of excitement
flowing over the surface of everything.
Maybe when it wisps into clouds
surging overhead it loses
itself in the shape of the wind.

Certainly, rock remembers
more ancient tales
than the oldest member
of the human tribe.

Matter is a labyrinth
in which the spirit meanders,
thwarting attempts
to be understood clearly,
a good-natured trickster
doffing different shapes
hopping into new states
laughing at our frail need
to hold things down.

The Face of the World Sees Itself

The face of the river glides, sliding quickly sideways downstream,
a flowing smile that slips by, gone before we can smile back.
The face of the man sleeping on the bench sinks into his dream,
yet first looks deeply into our memory where he will always rest.
The face of the open-handed child skipping past on the street
lifts up high, rises above our heads defining the future heaven.

The little faces of small things, forks, knives, doorknobs, wrenches
shelter themselves by lodging snugly in our everyday appreciative
    gaze,
yet the face of Chickies Rock, thrust up from Susquehanna river-
    bottom
millions of years ago is blank with dementia, forgetting its source.
The many new smaller things surround the old big blank ancient
    ones
circling them with gleaming eyes, so they see themselves in this
    regard.

The faces of snakes impassive are left to burrow into the earth,
    while
trees mirror the expressions of other trees to form the grand chorus
of a forest, as dark skies gloomily threaten, grimace like a
    menacing mob,
while white streaky clouds racing light-heartedly, keep open an eye
to look beyond where they are, as its many expressions gathered
make the Earth's face so long, we must journey far to catch its
    glance.

Myriad, multitude of faces looking, we also see through their
    miens,
each of our faces, as Virginia Woolf exhorts us, gains a thousand
    eyes.

Cézanne Wished to Grasp the Hands of Nature

Cézanne was a doctor of the landscape, who carefully prepared as
    if for surgery.

Days upon days, he would trace the veins and arteries underground,
studying maps and geological surveys, to see and feel how the
water moves from neighboring climes to quench the land's thirst
and soak its soul.

He saw the bones and how they formed a skeleton to support the
    weight.

Movements of the rocky plates would shift but lock their fingers
so that granite palms and limestone limbs beneath the soil held
steady the life that ran and slithered unknowingly across its heft.

He took the pulse and listened to how untiring was the heartbeat.

He would sit for hours by the edge of the field or meadow or forest
    and
watch the way the wind moves tall grass or the sunlight pushes its
    way
into remote corners to sprout juniper bushes or cypresses as they
    swayed.

He would observe whether the eyes could follow his finger move
    in circles.

The birds no longer noticed him after hours stock still and
    swooped
around his hunched shoulders and head, whirling and chasing,
    cheeping

as the sun's finger slowly drew a line in front of him quieting his
  mind.

He would no longer see a patient there but began to hum with this
  body.

The trees no longer above and about him, lifted him gently into
    their tops
as his blood flowed green and his heart felt its leaves shiver and
  wave,
his breath stretched now from the beginning of the brook to the far
  horizon.

Finally, his hands could reach into the body to fix it by following
  its need.

The brush moved quickly with the flight of the birds across his
canvas with the tumble of rocks in a wash, an upstroke of wheat
reaching for the sun, and circles from color to color with the spring
of an early rabbit fleeing.

Our First Glance at the Light

The first light shaft splinters,
but not like the rays from the sun at sunset,
cloud filtered, seeking
a place to rest for the night,
but instead bouncing all around the cheek,
tickling feathers of radiance,
fingers of white warmth,
flying under the newborn chin
promising that the orbs will soon awaken—
for the first light cannot yet be—
that first light of the beginning,
since the eye always
lingers in the dark.

But the gasp of the first breath
should warn that to be a human being,
means that even air
can pierce through
to the heart, as the onrush
of life shocks and hurts.
The shaking, reddened need
of the *aah* that tore open a hole in the air
remains woven like
an ever-spreading vine
in every wreath
of breath and sound.

The Gustatory Zeal of Falling Snow

As the towhee's cry is slurped up into stillness
by the white tongue of snow spreading serpentine
over cars and hills, as it fattens itself,
applies to surfaces, tastes oil slicks and marsh grass,
scotch pines and smoke from chimneys rising.

Where streaming rickety waters creak over
slumbering salamanders, they carve
a laceration in the white fervent skin,
but deftly done, to prevent snow from devouring
river and so halting the cannibal temptations
within the watery tribe.

A wooden church has never been so savory
to lost souls as it is to this tongue
that never wags in penitence,
nor has the old woman slipping in fear
at being insistently licked
felt for decades on her wrinkled skin
a caress driven to cover her completely
and melt with her.

The leftovers in the dumpster, the homeless
on the streets, the chemicals oozing from drains,
the mash of debris underfoot,
and the tears of the abandoned we are loathe to take
into our mouths and taste their plight
are swallowed completely without hesitation
by this seemingly cold winter,
who finds them all to be its sacrament.

Falling Echoes

Autumns themselves seem to pile up
like the leaves crunching underfoot,
kicked about,
then sliding across the sidewalk
in the wind
that suddenly insists.

The leaves want to hold on
and grab the at sidewalk
but they slide along and tumble.
It's too late
having left the tree,
they've fallen into the world and its cold,
like so many friends
who fell into the wind.

The fireplace conjures their faces,
flames pop indolently
and we hold hands
repeating their stories
making their souls
flicker again in the flames.

I see them flashing in your eyes
as we hold them together in
sighs and another tale.
We wrap ourselves
in their lingering
and in each other's arms
like a heavy Amish quilt.

Thomas Hobbes Denies Perception's Sense

Hobbes said that within hearts
and souls were gears and pulleys
moved by propelling atoms,
blind messengers
from the world who scurry
from mountain to eye
and liver to brain.
Seeming momentous inspirations
are only residues
of minute harried commuters
indifferent to their beginnings
and destinations.

Wars fought between tyranny
and freedom,
lovers finding light in lover's eyes,
artists carving in granite
ballet dancers pirouetting in stone,
poets finding remote canyons
confiding in whispers by walking
swaying word footbridges,
all these are just dramas of illusion,
afterimages
of energy exchanges
and bumping particles.

Hobbes loved
a woman of lavender eyes
who adored hyacinths,

but unlike Proust
the blossoms were not a church
or the key to belief,
but rather for Hobbes
a reason to distrust his heart
and call it a mere
rusting machine.

The Body So Fragile in Its Strength

The body so fragile in its strength
withstands blow after blow,
blasts of icy winds blue
with trying to blow out
its smoldering inner fire
while still burning
comfortingly warm

more miraculously
than the candles
in the surrounded holy temple
burning for eight days
on one day's oil,

not yielding to the flat fist
of concrete fallen upon,
an unexpected smash to the face
more of a dazzling right hook
than any from a boxer,

sending out battalions
of brave interior warriors
to repulse the invading germs
grimly intent on hijacking
the sweet charms of independent life,

even the implosion of organs or arteries
pledged to keep the flow moving
melodiously for decades
by accepting transplanted strangers
into its most intimate places
to be tutored into the right rhythms,

still gasping, struggling to hold its path
when betrayed by others of its kind,
other bodies who affront it with furious fists
or foreign objects of steel
shoved or shot into its heart.

City Walking on a Hot August Night

Even the sidewalk exhales
as the leftover heat of the day
returns to the sky, lifting without body
above trees to push stars
higher into their constellations.

The diffuse light left over
whispers from trees and grass
who can no longer speak
after the day's heat
forced a stoic silence.

Unspoken syllables suspended
in oppressive air
swim in lingering energy
filling the night
with a snaking glow.

Sounds of our feet
on sidewalk simmer,
not scrape, as moving
summer things melt and merge
in the late air.

Finding a way out of the
clinging grasp of afternoon,
its hands all over our bodies.
we welcome the cool distance
of respecting stars.

II. Shared Bodies of Nature

The Torn Ozone Layer

We believe only humans can rip open the sky
through our genius with minds so special
our inventions pierce the atmosphere
to create a display of glory above,
when really we create sluggish brown smog
rising from factories we lack the will to fix,
eating holes in the planet's wrap.

Painful to have punched a hole in
what really is planetary love,
though we think it smart to say *ozone,*
not realizing this is the combined care
of the creatures who exhale
fervor for one another.
Plants sing arias to steadfast trees
while these old sentinels, thankful
for melodies at their feet,
send mists of joy shrouding their leafy tops,
before it ascends ever higher.
A blanket of atoms of affection
slipping over nature's bodies
who lie in the bower of the planet.

This invisible quilt is sewn
by the real wizards
of our planet, since true magic
occurs when so many achieve
a mutual embrace
it encircles each one
as it fills the sky.

No Time for Goodbyes

the birds and the bees were messengers
in the stories our parents told us
to usher in life's secrets.

Gone are hordes of bees who flew
in circles where each erratic dip
says more than our words.
Grains of pollen added melodiously
to the brewing of honey
in the buzzing of a thousand cooks
working on the same recipe
in the concentrated hum of their hives,
doing so many tasks seamlessly
when humans would bump and stumble,
caught in clashing gears of egos.

Without the charming Eros of bees
kissing every sugary flower's stamen,
a sexual slurp not driven by conquest
or driven by the need to be affirmed,
but arising from the sheer joy in color
and of sweetness on the tongue,
then crops will not shoot up to wave
in the wind, and the noisy planet's
teeming crowd will cease, whether rhinos
in mud baths or New Yorkers at clubs.

Our childhood songs promised bluebirds
faithfully sitting on our windowsill
announcing the good day come
since their blue was like the sky
endlessly wrapped in bright sun.
Now there is no herald by the pane
and only the friends of Audubon
in some lonely spot hear their song.

                    II.

princes were to come to princesses
in the guise of frogs to be kissed.

A missing note startles us awake
at the silence of the bog across the way,
where past the reeds, the water-skippers
flap their arms noiselessly in mime,
as if begging for the reggae rhythm
that kept time in a chorus of croaks.
The frogs had seemed like the grass
sprouting in any open space or watery den.
Frog love was urgent as the summer
and missing its chorus the hot night
no longer offers us the moon.

The Trees Speak

We do not fear death as we take in light
changing its glow into waving spirits
leaping from our branches long before
the falling leaves that follow.

We stand in silent meditation for decades
of inner retreat, spreading calm
like a fine mist until the planet
steadies on the axis of our dream.

A rhythm borrows from the resolve
knotted within our trunks as we quietly
look upon you chaotic younger siblings,
as you lunge against each other,

rending yourselves, unless we can
guide you into a circular path
like the birds we show the way home
from spring into fall.

We touch sky and draw upon the earth
gathering others into a sheltering bower,
a pirouette from root to prayer, sky
to branch, a space where eyes find rest.

We lose limbs, suffer insects burrowing
into flesh, blights devour whole continents
of our families, but we stay upright,
grateful for the reach of remaining branches.

We practice loss each fall
as stripped to the humility of bare
grey wrinkled skin unable to hide
our blemishes or old scars.

Even in your war with our species,
we are silent when companions are cut
into the slabs of lost consciousness
of the simpler moments on this planet.

Our bodies are sawed, nailed together,
painted, unnoticed in what you call home
while we hold the planet on its course
hoping you find your lost roots.

Auden, Making Promises May Not Be Better

"Let them leave language to their lonely betters."
—W. H. Auden

We do anything to avoid her, yet she is the mother of all things,
the slinking stealthy wolf, the steps of the heron's stairway of air
lazily leaving the river, the hummingbird peeking into the skirts
of the red flower, the Mandeville climbing with slow sinew
of the sun lifting its green reach. All coming in quiet to the
       company
of those who know the spring watering this world is silence.

Even though the wolf howls in concert in the deep night,
the heron can be startled into a cry, the twirl of tiny wings does
       hum,
the plants can very lightly rustle when plucked by the wind,
yet in finding ways to feed, love and play, each comes to rest
within the soundless circle that is wider than any collection
of words or sounds from which they borrow their heart.

The Naked Oyster's Rondeau Redoublé

Into a small shell, many things will crawl.
Full-grown, not needing shelter, still
an aging oyster, bruised from a fall
comes back, dragging its drooping will.

to sit inside again, secure. Shaking,
crouched by the fire, huddled by the wall,
sits the oyster and watches, as quaking
into a small shell, many things will crawl.

Squid and eels, worms and sponges, dazed by blows,
come staggering up to the well-stocked still
and swagger a bit, and hope it shows.
Full-grown, not needing shelter, still

just stopping by for a drink, they
put on airs, boast, and try to look tall.
The fishy features quiver, but still look gay.
An aging oyster, bruised from a fall

broods over his drink and nods to all.
He knows what lurks beneath flapping gill.
He's seen too many a fish with proud drawl,
comes back dragging its drooping will.

An aging oyster has had time to think,
and knows that many a hook will cut and tear,
and that all sea creatures will at times sink.
Nodding he knows, sometimes all crawl bare
                    into a small shell.

Getting Lost in January Woods

Working hard for weeks,
this day declared amnesty from effort
those woods no one knew
who owned them, stretching
from winding narrow road
towards the Sound,
yet no one ever arrived at a shore
just always towards it.

Astride a log, tightening leather laces
to boots, pulled tight with a sigh
loosens breath too long held
in measured rhythm,
looking deep into the trees
who trail away
oblivious to direction or purpose
sunk within their musings.

Striding along, pulled by the magnet
of trees who seem to stand in place,
yet move from here to there
since the columns of trees
birth currents flows between trunks
by pointing towards where quiet
is so dense it runs
deep into a well we seek.

Wandering from tree to tree
listening for the secret call
of those who declare and move
without losing the calm of place
watching for a sweeping limb
to point to the disappearing trail
my mind evanesces into the mist
on the afternoon snowy ground.

As cold dark comes between
the trees and the sky, falling slow,
winding among the paths
and whisperingly swallowing the day,
a fear of becoming invisible
among the still ones of winter night
propels my feet to find
the way back from enchantment.

The Hunted Demon Is the Most Social Animal

A wolf craves muzzle to muzzle, yips echoed
by the white furred dancing partner of its life,
as they run in the same track through the night.

A wolf craves rolling on its back
feeling the soft weight of another angular head
on its chest, their loosed jaws inhaling
the frigid night air as they lie on the snow
curled together, long paths already traveled
in a loping trot that never tires.

Even at sixty below zero, the cold ground
reassures them as they sink into its embrace
feeling the heat of the heart of the planet
keenly even at this distance
its flames shine in the embers of their eyes.

Moving farther than any creature on the planet
hours glide by silently in their steady tread
as they sail over the land atop the snow
in the dark gliding like ships in full sail
with the prow of their snout into the wind
devouring miles in a long circle back home.

II

Back by their den, they chase the snowflakes
like confetti, and race full tilt towards each other
charging, feinting, biting with teeth tucked under,
yapping and rolling together, playing paws
held aloft waving like babies' hands, as a
silent glee fills the valley bouncing off trees.

Even the crow is enchanted enough
to inch forward towards the prancing spirits,
inching closer to the jaws that nip at its tail
lunging in mock attack,
crows cawing in guffaws, wolves racing
wildly towards it a hundred times,
until the they fall over panting.

Another baby-sitting older grey
bumps the pups who chase and bite,
battle and butt in endless
growling charges of barks and howls,
before all their elders have collapsed
after taking their turn joining
in the laughter of generations.

There are no lone wolves, hardened
like the ice of the tundra, but only
wolves missing the snuggling of family,
their pack, as they hotly pursue the scents
to find those with whom
they might spend days in play.

III

Many tribes tell how the caribou and elk
were sad as on the windswept ice
as many would lie down to die too early
with hollow eyes of hunger seeking
even a green tuft to eat, unable to deny any
their place in the grazing herd.

The Great Spirit sent down the wolves
to charge amidst the caribou, once, twice
and a third time until the bent one of age
or with bloody cough came forward
to look the wolves in the eye, starting
a long silent talk between them.

No doubt the old or sick elk would stare
at its end and reassure the wolf it was ready
to leave the herd coming forward
for the sake of all, as they watch still as evergreens
the old one run forward to join a wider circle
of life and death.

The wolves understand the logic of a pack,
and make quick work of their feast,
eating every smattering, until a few hairs remain
knowing no morsel of sacrifice
should go wasted, not mad with bloodlust,
but quick and sure
in closing the link of life to life.

The Wolf Asks, *Who Is the Demon?*

The Medieval Europeans declared wolves to be
devils, fiends with blood smeared mouths,
gulping down the innocent creatures of the earth.
Yet, humans force the staggering line of cattle
forward with crackling prods, shuffled ahead
to be seared by hundreds of thousands of volts
and hung upside down to bleed to death.

Humans show proudly pictures of thousands
of wolf carcasses nailed to the side of sheds
in a seemingly never-ending line, some two million
shot, clubbed, poisoned to avenge their supposed
depraved ways, while we virtuous ones
fly above in helicopters shooting those
whose joy at end of day is to gather and sing.

Auden insisted we were their lonely betters
who promise, living in the holiness of the word,
yet perhaps humans should try to be like those
who stay with their kin for life, mourning the loss
of any member of the pack for months
with tails down and their cries rending the sky.

Birdfeeder Doubts

Toes dig, almost slip,
mince across icy paving stones
carry the bag of black oiled sunflower seeds
to the swaying feeder,
frozen grass flat with odd curly wisps
of greenish tan blades
bundled by the cold wind
and I ask myself
the real reason for this gift.

Do I admire the tough flitting spirit
of those wrens who fly through the cold
while I retreat beside my wood stove fire,
so much, they must be honored,
fed as if family members
or do my resonating bones recall
scrawny ancestors in frigid caves?

Maybe, it is selfish food
for my hungry eyes
sick of brown,
waiting for the joy
of the red diagonal burst
of the cardinal who blasts the gloom
of the March muddy yard
into a canvas set ablaze
by crimson pulled out
from everything's hidden fire.

Feeder's broken sides cracked open
by razor surfaced squirrel tooth attack,
launched in fear of winter's fallow spread,
yet the shaking marauders' sides
bulge with summer glut
like scurrying well-fed humans
who feel there is never enough.

Remembering Canid Nights

The fire crackles as they come out of the dark trees,
their eyes red mirrors ringing the outer circle
just beyond reach,
just beyond imagining.

Drawn out of the forest by wafting clouds
of campfire cooking, smoky smell of heaven,
paw placed before paw, inching,
like edging down a rope.

They whine with that high note of hunger
that makes the gaunt human mothers
searching too for food
look with tears at their thin babies.

Wolves bone-know how their howling
at packs of other humans lets the prone shapes
of this pack settle further into the ground,
sigh for the safety won in leaving them scraps.

At day's break, they flit through
the sunny air, a night's dream dissipated,
trotting easily for miles
in their other life.

Scientists are amazed that they evolved so fast
from the wild to the willed, from the outside
to alongside, canine and human hip
pressed together beneath blankets.

Dogs still keep the pact, paw to hand,
to guard against intruders, but we
foolishly hope they forget the electricity
of runs through woods after prey.

Forgetting their gallop and snarl kept us alive
added their ears and fangs to our weak flesh.
The same hair-trigger blaze in them
also chases swirling snowflakes with glee.

Bhakti, the Zen Chihuahua

She came from Paradise, not the celestial,
but the place with black Amish buggies
with red flags waving,
warning the twenty-first century to slow down,
with boys in rounded hats hammering quietly
using old barn wood to interlock smoothly,
their tongues tied and looking stoically handsome.

Maybe, it was those shining eyes without words
taught her to be still, not barking for a year,
but even at sixteen able to calm a room.
Her big brown eyes had moons in them
seeming to hold fast a heavenly tide
to guide her serenely through bustle.

She was named for that dog
first and only animal
to enter Nirvana,
since Yudhishthira,
gambler of kingdoms and brides,
but, oh so holy, wouldn't
leave behind his most loyal friend.
Brahman at the gates couldn't believe
he wouldn't enter without her,
until Brahman fathomed
the depth of a dog's heart.

Poets Like Others Ignorant About Turtles

I.

We think turtles are slow,
dimwitted and humorless,
yet if you for millennia were teased,
maligned and misunderstood,
how then dance a jig
rather become solemn-eyed
and seek protection within yourself.

Here is another otherwise fine poem
bemoan the stolid character
of the turtle, the poet horrified to imagine,
stacked on top of each other,
turtles down to the earth's core,
the essence of the planet
an amalgamation of terrapin scorn.

Yet, having lived for decades
with these pleasant mates,
I wonder what other creatures
on this fair planet can sing songs,
make love, form communities, soundlessly?

Modern humans trust that rushing about
evokes fiery forces from the sky,
deluded that creating electricity
where there was once stillness
is a boon to the planet,
that making atoms shake and split apart
is better than respecting their tiny integrity.

The disparaged turtle stack
is marvelous considerateness,
turtle on turtle on turtle,
each spirit so attuned to the others
gravity can't find any dissension
with which to pull them down.

II.

The turtle's head at a rising angle
pointing up and seemingly stopped
in mid-reach towards action and bold speech
is not the human pause of self-absorption
but attention so fine, the fly
skimming the pond a world away
dances in its eye and resounds
in the quiet space of its shell,
acoustic resonance finer than
any Philharmonic hall.

Two turtles below water,
her eyes seeing green, his flippers
becoming delicate conductor's hands
waving gently before her nose
motioning a watery need
to join rocking together in the current,
where is the human serenade to compare?

Yet, when she swims mockingly away
he does not get a gun or even burrow
under rocks to brood, but swims
faster than any finny fish, strong arms
loving the water's slippery support,
and seems happily to sink to bottom
to meditate for hours with Buddha's half-smile,
which makes me ask
which species
has a sense of humor?

Hummingbirds Signal the Evolution of Mind

The hummingbird barely seems to be
where it is, so quickly jerked aside,
we blink and wonder.
But the hummingbird wing beats
count out the pulsing rhythm
we knew when our thoughts flashed
in the neural hemisphere's theater
flickering thousands of time faster
than our slow minds now trundle.

Our minds used to whir as fast
as hummers drunk on color
and were drunk, too,
turning our eyes here and there,
lost looking in the sky,
glances lighting on branches,
sipping the sweetness of everything.

We could never get enough,
foraged all day to see more.

Every few thousand years,
a teacher comes to place
soothing hands on our chests,
sounds the drum of the earth,
tells us to stop our frenzy.

Turtles were left behind
as examples
for our minds might slow
and begin to look breathingly
at the forest as we raise our heads
to face our interlocutors
and pool purpose within.

The lessons left over eons,
thoughts were to be shepherded
to move deliberately
to inch ever further beyond
the mountain edge
to gather carefully like the mist
in wispy air where the peaks follow
the line of their green backs
towards sunlight
and evaporate in pale colors
for a moment caught in the wan light
to bow to all things.

Speaking the Same Language

With electronic gadgets and wired homes
left far behind, we begin to find
our way after weeks by the angle
of the sun through high saluting
branches, by tracing the silent hike
of stars through limbs of light,
by following salamanders
slipping down the stream's steps.

We all share signs with bees
who pirouette the news of flowers
found sun directed,
with geese still flying after dark
in the wake of constellations,
and even the black bear watches
the smallest creatures
going downhill towards winter sleep.

The Natural Power of Memory

The Clark's nutcracker knows where every seed
is stored in tree burrows and beneath wedged rock outcrops,
thousands and thousands of them
as if they were the words of an immense novel
and each one linked with the others to tell a hopeful story
that in reading and rereading,
paying attention to the tale,
it can survive the harsh months of blank windswept grounds
where no comforting messages can be discerned
flying above.

It's a hidden hieroglyphic of an old avian myth
to get through winters
that each bird writes in thistles and seeds
to leave its own Ariadne's thread
through swaying evergreens and crackling pines.
It's an unfinished composition of wings and beaks
through generations of hatchlings
knowing the Braille of the land
and the grammar of the sky
and the perfect pitch of the seasons
that only a Homer, Tolstoy or Beethoven
can leave for us secreted
in the midst of our winter.

Blue Holes in the Cosmic Fabric

Black holes lie beyond vision and regular rules of thought
to lurk within what is unfindable,
a nothing where something should be
and yet is so utterly nothing
that even the light of day
loses its way forward,
even though its distinct path
defines what is forward.
Our scientists can imagine these black holes
since the negative and what's missing
are the modern norm—to multiply
them forever and utterly was easy,
even if it's impossible
to multiply zero infinitely,
and arrive at the non-place
where nothing escapes or shows itself.

Yet, the universe is actually more riddled
with blue holes that spring up
whenever heartfelt connection ebbs,
leaving an infinitesimal place
where vibrant love remains
circling in the color of the sky filled with light
but refracted by human care,
tiny cerulean dreams unable to dissipate
leaving eddies of joy between those who look
into each other's eyes, feeling a pull
so strong it never loses its hold
on our center of gravity.

When a Body Moves Through Space

When a body moves through space
    the world turns on its axis
        leaving abruptly
       lingering conversations among oceans
in deep tectonic voices
    whispering secrets
            only known by those
who close their eyes
    to the come-on gesturing
       of the lonely in soft isolated beds
         who are afraid to sink into the earth
          while walking shoeless through
    the loamy desire of ferns and moles.

The bodies allowed to bathe in loamy lust
    open their skin to the pressing
       caress of silent trees and rock
  and clouds
       that get under and go within the flesh,
    labyrinths of labyrinths
       or pomegranates of pomegranates
      seeds stacked up to burst fluidly
       showering flavor on tongues
  that need not reveal
    that the moving of sensual bodies
      upon other bodies
       sounds the deepest note of all.

Practicing the Tao

Go back to the uncarved block,
slide a hand over the grain
of raw wood
and read the Braille
of the trees' sighs.
Move silently to the low point
beneath the hill
remembering the rays of sun,
long ribbons
entangling the child.

No Thought

Caressing your back, the hand unclasps
in joy at being home
in a haven like a sheltered pond,
or like our bed at night,
a perfect declivity
where it belongs
nestled in without a thought
of where to go.
The hand smooths the surface
of the waters that flow within you,
as my eye happily floats upon
the ripples of your lovely curves.
I lightly swirl in a current
that propels me
for the rest of the day
without effort
as my busy plans sink
into muddy silt
where they belong.

I was twelve years old running
in full stride
as the ball calls me into embrace
like the dancer catching
his partner in her fall into the air.
I still feel it join the flight of my legs
and arms and hands in a movement
that never ends,
like hiking steps across gnarled logs
over crashing streams
that join legs pumping
seemingly forever
in my sojourn.

These meetings linger within,
propel the circle of dancing horses
of my childhood,
push along gently at their backs
on the body's carousel of affection.
These horses are not the wooden
or painted ones, but made out
of a rhythm that turns me
towards each day.

Proust's Pirouette

Marcel, the dreamer,
sees the moonlight as
an enchanted ladder
reaching down for us to ascend
into places where the silver glow
shines on dormant bodies
who would be dancers,

spinning perhaps on treetops
while leaves wave with
the rhythm of regret
in frayed sidelong signs
of lost hopes
until this instant.

Longings who waited
for years practicing together
at the barre of desire
in the glistening night
hoping that dreams
might turn them into dance

take the floor
after these years of yearning
while the feeble mind
climbs out from
the too bright
prison of fact.

Seals Sail by All Day at Cape Cod

The old Navajos say birds endure
by entering the wind.
I watch seals swim by
as the ocean streams steadily
up the coast like a watery gale.

The seals bob up and down
as if on an enormous, submerged carousel
encircling the globe,
not swimming but riding
on the deep currents

that offer free admission
since nature does not love to hide
as Heraclitus mistakenly declared.
Nature instead takes all others
on its back.

The Body Between Us

They say the body separates
as if a galactic span
intrudes between glances
intertwined limbs, desires,
your hand in mine,
a frozen continent of flesh
within flesh
without light.

Yet, your fingers lightly
brushing my back aflame
is a Shakespearian sonnet
of metaphors leaping
in blood and nerves
from hand to heart
polysyllabic beyond
any writer's ken.

The Body of the One I Love

The pull of the body of the one I love
ever increases
beckons to undiscovered places
to linger, meander
across her body
offering paths
through sheltering alcoves
of her kind and softening curves,
a moment of breathing in completely,
slow moment of solace
and renewal.

The concavity of her hip sings
a song of intrigue
that somehow
I must have rushed by
or maybe it emerged
on those long runs together
or maybe I learned
to really see
what is all around me.

Her eyes were always deep
with promises
circles of resonance
with tides of the earth
and winds moving
among all creatures,
lines we cross in our rhythm
as we know each mood,
touch still opens worlds of steps
altering the dance
of intimacy.

Her body invites vigorously
as I cherish flows followed before
noticing their art snug against me.
Familiar meetings
with one loved so long
fires the skin translucent
with need to join the one
who cares so much
the night flickers with thousands
of firefly acts of kindness.

The Body Becomes

The body becomes
a guide who shepherds
the spirits of those who lived
before me into my blood,
circling a heart beating
still with their rhythms,
breathing still with their concerns,
reaching still with their hands,
finding their words
still ringing in my ears.

The body becomes
a place where I reach
for stars whose rays
travel here from a galaxy
full of cascading notes
of pure harmonies reverberating
within their light
infusing my gestures
with a symphonic power
over this inherited land.

The body becomes
a station through which
speed the dreams
of those I love signaling
to the world their will
walks through my steps
gathering me into a larger
dance of purpose
where each fluid gesture
welcomes others.

Élan Vital Proliferates

A steady pulse draws from black earth
momentum of worms industriously burrowing
or water rising from deep hidden places
shared by fungus networks as trees talk
silently, aiding one another in arboreal compassion
for those in their families who are failing.

A wolf lying on the ground, ribs pressed lengthwise,
held firmly between above and below,
charged enough to lope for miles and miles.
electrified by currents in roots of grass spliced
into fibers running everywhere below our steps
sparks spreading among vegetal beings.

In the backyard, a grandchild smears red goop
over its fingers in four-year old delight,
slurping love across the white paper
as his heart says *I miss sitting in your lap, grandpa,*
feeling the grass tingle with a millennial desire
to bind the things of the earth into a weave.

The grandad's thighs, a steady catchment basin,
still pool his cares in the old man's lap,
a runoff from a line of dads and sons,
and a sweetheart or two, who held onto
the back of his neck as he looked out
over mountains winking in the distance.

Becoming Their Silhouette

I thought the idea
was mine
until the yellow finch
dropped onto the apple
tree branch
swiveled its head,
aimed its arrow of vision
black eyed
entering my hazel gaze.

I thought the fear
was mine
hands icy despite rays of sun
as screeching, the squirrel
frenzied itself
through mazes of limbs
seeing the red-tailed hawk
circling
red moon returning.

I thought the care
was mine
until hushed slow
slipping through the woods
fawns flitted
green mossy ground
found
silky doe waiting
nestling them to belly.

I thought the peace
was mine
long reward
of seeking, ceasing
but the cumulus cloud
sliding cobalt neighborhood
open air
almost weightless
knowingly
borrowed light
from surrounding sky.

I can see the me
is not mine
scattered in leaves,
acorns,
seed for birds,
rising air
nestled among furbearers,
carried by frenetic nesters
settling back into the iris.

Entropy and Ecstasy

An engine not running at a hundred percent efficiency
frustrates the engineer slumped beside the thumping machine,
his nineteenth century desire for perfection thwarted
by some invisible hand of the universe poking his heart
with millions of tiny impish escaping waves of heat fleeing.

This flight was a personal insult, an occasion for mourning,
when Boltzmann named the movement of energy as *heat loss*
since these men wanted it to stay in a metal box working away
like their sorely missed fathers who worked until they dropped
or their former wives who left needing respite inspired by care.

Yet the molecules were actually sensitive to the greater lack
of energy and life outside the steely chamber and were not
abandoning their job but feeling the compelling pull
to flow through walls of confinement in a surge of freedom
and answer the invitation to enter the larger world.

The *motional* tendency of molecules was decried by Boltzmann
as *heat waste* since the control of their energies had slipped
through his fingers like so many he had loved in vain, or so
he and many like him felt, was wasted energy when others left
through their own differing wills or through the zero of death.

It could be energy or particles that moved out of the place
where they had been decreed to spend their days being productive
that the men of the next century called *disorder* resenting
the *breakdown,* as they saw it, of the order they built
to stay safe and make sure that there were no sudden changes.

Those molecules were attracted to joining up with others
in need of connection and interaction, new communities
that gained heat or energy or more substance when formerly
they had been poorer and now had more life and might
even with these newcomers transform into something new.

As for those molecules, they had gone beyond themselves,
ec-static, which means to step beyond where one had been,
joyously overflowing the boundaries others had imposed
so, one could be counted upon and given a definite name,
but instead, they burst their old skins to open new eyes.

Of Squash and Creation

We planted squash for years
tendrils snaked along the grass
overriding the flimsy fence
of chicken wire and stakes
with stars of yellow blooms
reaching in all directions
shouting *plenty to come*
to any who would listen
yet always a silent
shriveled collapse,
not one zucchini dared
come forth into being.

In this year of people hiding,
their viral breath now toxic,
their hugs no longer
a sign of care,
become a push of others
into fear of the plague,
the squash reach out
everywhere,
engulfing tomatoes,
burying basil,
flying across the yard
and climbing fences,
blooming,
offering fruits
beyond counting.

That moment when enemies
become sudden friends,
when storms leave
to open a cool sky,

when cancers ravage
then surprisingly remit,
when in this instant
we feel these quick changes
from despair to hope,
from hate to love,
from death to rebirth,
to *voila,*
as the chrysalis
takes flight,
this is an echo of that
original millisecond when void
bursts into matter.

God was the name
for this instant,
now called
the *big bang*
as if there would be
terrible noise
suddenly
in the vast silence,
but the silence
remains faithfully still
in birth,
not coming from outside
by a Creator
nor announced loudly
as everything
comes to be,
but rather change
is the embrace of a quiet
we dream.

The Body Is

The body goes unnoticed
its trillions of little workers
in purring perfection
like the bees in a hive
feeds me too
like the honey
keeps me here
among the purple petunias
my dogs licking my legs,
they fly across the yard
onto my chair,
below me my wife reaches down,
shapely body suddenly
in front of my ravished eyes
and kisses me quietly.

The body gives me a place
to be among all these things,
for whom I awake
in the morning with a start
slipping into the overgrown woods
by the path following
the Susquehanna lazily along,
later the smell
of the morning coffee
slides into me
a comforting hand of greeting
as my wife's eyes open to a sky
green through the trees
surrounding our window
reflected in her eyes where
they have a home.

Is It Lost?

Is it lost when struck like a tuning fork my body resonates
with the mallards' feet dancing on the river's face?

Is it lost when seeing the blue of an indigo bunting opens
my eyes to a masterful palette within the green field?

Is it lost when the frisson flying down my spine hearing
the right f-sharp unlocks a syncopation with my lover?

Is it lost when the aroma of bread baking on a frosty
morning allows my hunger to thaw?

Is it lost when touching my lover's skin its translucence
lets me see the movement of worlds within?

Is it lost when my lover tucks into my arm at night
smoothing the wavy surface of my dreams?

Or do bursts of feeling dive deep below to settle
in the unfathomable silt in a Lethe of mind?

Could instants felt weave a circle of sense to put
me in a world I would otherwise lose?

The Temporal Taste of the Buddha's Strawberry

A sunlit walk through the forest as creatures rejoice
in the warmth moving through the air of their bodies
when seeing a shaking camelia leaf freezes his step,
a growl adds a base note to the song of the nearby stream.

The sudden cold gripping his heart betrays
a tiger will leap through the forest's circle of peace
driven by hunger as then both silently begin to run
over leaves and trunks, swept into an unseen torrent.

Coming to the edge of a cliff, the man's racing feet
pedal furiously flailing in the air amidst the blue
he falls into, as his hands grabbing, find a green vine
and he hangs in the still air looking at a cliff face.

In a crevice, a little green snake of a shoot holds
by a thread, yet within reach, a swollen strawberry.
The vision of his mother in a saffron sari offers
a bowl of this fruit as his father shakes his head:

He must become a warrior to fight the forest,
slay wild tigers and make our enemies tremble.
Yet he sits quiet in the sun and loves strawberries
as if they were more precious than our jewels.

The Buddha knew without looking below the ledge
another pacing tiger awaited inflamed with fury,
like in his father, yet he smiles at his mother's face
as he reaches for the ripe berry, slurping its juice.

Shining eyes accompany sweetness on his tongue,
he hears the tabla and sitar of the palace musicians,
feels supple muscles supporting him atop Kanthaka
smells the loamy earth of fields he endlessly walked.

He lives a life and many more in that moment when
succulent strawberry juice suffuses within tides
of time the myriad caresses of all things and
the loving glances of all the souls he met.

Lascaux's Echoing

Deep recesses, dark cave, water singing its way down
long cavern walls, a rock scrapes rock wall, leaving
its imprint, held by a shaggy hand, whose heart runs
alongside the deer, the horses, and aurochs to the wind.

The hand seeks not to capture or even picture, but feel
kin of the forest moving under the silence of the night
dark shapes winding about sentinel oaks to hide
from wolves in the same fall cold forewarning winter.

Swabbing the red, yellow, tan and black onto stone
smeared with fat and clay, the iron oxide became
the hands' voice of many notes of a praise sung
to tell next generations who belongs to their family.

The animals on the cave wall leave their mooring
in limestone and begin to run when seen in the eyes
of those who live with them, so humans too can feel
the ground flow beneath hooves in pounding stride.

Even more, the circling cluster of white stars and moon
casts streaks of light on trees entering auroch, horse,
deer hearts in the wildfire of being alive in the cold night,
passed on to enthralled cave dwellers as art's shock.

Gusts of Wind and Time

Sailing on the bay yesterday, the strong thrust of the wind
seems to be gathered from everywhere in the sky
as if the blue had invisible hands coming from behind
in a comforting push on my back on that playground swing.

Those many years ago, I wanted to go higher than the sky
and not come down and ride the bus for hours to my weekend
visit to my divorced father in Philly or land in the circle
of Gerritsen Beach bullies who beat me for being a Jew.

The water swells on the boat's hull propel me further
from those days of hiding in the landfill weeds
behind the handball courts, while my crew of current
friends has no idea of the port I am leaving behind.

Heading on a different bearing late in life after sailing
around the globe, the gliding current guides me through
time's swaying buoys in the joy of slipping beyond the past
through waves where wind gusts blow the spray of now.

About the Author

Glen A. Mazis taught philosophy and humanities for decades at Penn State Harrisburg and retired in the summer of 2020. He has published more than 90 poems in literary journals, including *Rosebud, The North American Review, Sou'wester, Spoon River Poetry Review, Willow Review, The Atlanta Review, Reed Magazine,* and *Asheville Poetry Review* (best of 1994–2004). His poetry collection, *The River Bends in Time,* was published by Anaphora Literary Press in March 2012, and his chapbook, *The Body Is a Dancing Star,* was published by Orchard Street Press in 2020. His poem won the 2019 Orchard Street Press National Poetry contest [The Malovrh-Fenlon Prize].

He is also the author of five books of cultural critique and philosophy: *Emotion and Embodiment; The Trickster, Magician and Grieving Man: Returning Men to Earth; Earthbodies: Rediscovering Our Planetary Senses; Humans/Animals/Machines: Blurring Boundaries;* and *Merleau-Ponty and the Face of the World: Silence, Ethics, Imagination and Poetic Ontology.*

Mazis is a marathon runner, a hiker, a Zen meditator, the Borough Council President, a gardener, and a beginning sailor of a 1976, 30-foot sailboat, named Merleau (French: "*Mer*" is "sea" and "*L'eau*" is "water"; hence, "Seawater"). Mazis loves the natural world and all its creatures, lives happily with his wife Judith, also a poet, and their two dogs, Sophie and Rosie, alongside the Susquehanna River.

www.ingramcontent.com/pod-product-compliance
Ingram Content Group UK Ltd.
Pitfield, Milton Keynes, MK11 3LW, UK
UKHW010221200625
6476UKWH00053B/238